How To Get The Most Out Of Your Lawyer

You'll Both Be Happier

by

Bruce I. Petrie

Illustrated by

Donald R. Heyl

How To Get The Most Out Of Your Lawyer
You'll Both Be Happier

by

Bruce I. Petrie

Cartoons and Design by Donald R. Heyl

Published by Sapiozoic Press
Cincinnati, Ohio

Printed in the United States of America
ISBN 0-9720219-0-6
Library of Congress Control Number 2002191134

How To Get The Most Out Of Your Lawyer

CONTENTS

APPENDIX

LAWYER
IN A
CAN
SEE INSTRUCTIONS
ON LABEL

How to Get The Most Out of Your Lawyer[1]
You'll Both Be Happier

FOREWORD

Unlike many purchases, professional services don't come with a set of instructions. Every new automobile is accompanied by an elaborate user's manual, pain pill packages include carefully phrased dosage limitations and warnings, cans of paint come with helpful hints on the label. But lawyers, who are among the most expensive purchases one is likely to make, often come bereft of useful information as to how they are to be utilized for maximum advantage. Therein lies the source of much dissatisfaction over the cost of such services.

Given the commonplace frustration with lawyers and legal problems, you may wonder why you should worry about helping a lawyer do his work. The simple answer of this booklet is: Because he is *your* lawyer and *you* pay his fees.

What follows is a distillation of fifty years of experience in the general practice of law in a midwestern American city, Cincinnati, Ohio to be exact, a city of about the right size to typify lawyers in the large cities as well as the small towns of the United States.

The cartoons are by Don Heyl, a Cincinnatian who is not a lawyer and thus could easily find some humor to add to this very serious subject.

If lawyers came in cans, you might find these instructions on the label.

Bruce I. Petrie

[1] For the sake of continuity, the same lawyer figure is pictured throughout this book and, therefore, to avoid confusion male pronouns are used in the text. Many lawyers are women and no substantive distinction is intended.

PICK YOUR
LAWYER
TRIAL LAWYER
CORPORATE LAWYER
PERSONAL INJURY
REAL ESTATE
BUSINESS LAWYER
1 CHANCE per person
PICK YOUR
LAWYER

FIRST, FIND THE RIGHT LAWYER - ONE SIZE DOESN'T FIT ALL

Finding a lawyer is easy. Finding the right lawyer is not so easy. It depends on the nature of your problem, e.g., wills and trust, real estate transaction, tax question. Asking a corporation lawyer to handle a personal injury case is like asking an orthopedic surgeon to remove your gall bladder.

Lawyers have come late to concentration on particular types of practice but are now there, forced by ever-increasing complexity. If it makes you feel better, you can blame lawyers themselves for the complexity or the plethora of new statutes (but it's a myth, incidentally, that lawyers comprise a majority of your state legislators).

You will save time and money by choosing a lawyer who fits the problem. Most medium to large sized firms will do that for you and you should not hesitate to ask for a lawyer who is expert on your type of problem. Your particular needs may also be satisfied by a small firm or a sole practitioner, but you must ask questions and seek references to make sure there is a fit. When in doubt, call a knowledgeable friend or the local Bar Association.

Despite the trend, some generalists remain. If your legal problems are various, ranging, say, from business issues to estate planning, try to stay within one firm and engage one lawyer who will have an overview of all of your problems and will call on colleagues when needed.

A ROSE IS NOT ALWAYS A ROSE

Keep in mind that from the day he's admitted to practice, every law graduate can call himself a lawyer (some seem to prefer "attorney"). But, for your purposes, you may not want a lawyer who is a politician with a law degree, or is more comfortable with influence than he is with law books or who thinks of himself as essentially a businessman (perhaps because he uses many business techniques to manage his practice).

Question him about his experience with your type of problem, ask him how much of the work he will do personally and how much he will assign to others in his firm, ask about progress reports to you and your getting a "second opinion" on crucial issues. If other professionals, e.g., accountants or engineers, will be collaborating with him, make sure that each role is defined and how each professional is to be paid. Most assuredly question him about his fees, as more fully discussed below. It is advisable that all this information be put in an engagement letter from him to you to avoid misunderstanding.

Time and Advice
Widgets
A. LINCOLN
ATTORNEY AT LAW

ACCORDING TO ABE,
TIME AND ADVICE ARE WORTH AS MUCH AS WIDGETS

If you are like most people dealing with a lawyer, his fees are often foremost in your mind. Except when representing plaintiffs in personal injury cases, (often compensated on a percentage basis) there are very few ways for a lawyer to anchor legal fees except by keeping track of the time spent and putting a value on each hour based upon the quality and experience behind your lawyer's advice. The resulting total may be adjusted up or down, but time is the basic factor.

Ask up front for his hourly rate and anticipated time. But realize the amount of time is usually very difficult to estimate, especially because you, rather than the lawyer, may be the cause of delays. Remember that much of his work will occur out of your presence. Remember also that the practice of law has become much more capital intensive, with computers, fax machines, multi-featured phone service, etc., all designed to help give you better service, but expensive.

Keep in mind that your lawyer's ability is the result of long years of education and hard work; that the law is constantly changing, meaning that his learning never ceases; that its value to you may well be hard to quantify but no less real, and the benefit may well be intangible and not appear until years later. Abe Lincoln, much longer a practicing lawyer than President, said it best: "A lawyer's time and advice are his stock in trade." Keep Abe in mind when you seek legal advice.

KEEP OFF THE GRASS

“DE MINIMIS NON CURAT LEX” MEANS WHAT IT SAYS

It’s been around since the Romans: “The law does not concern itself with trifles”. Even some wrongs that could be cured by the law should not be. They are too trivial to bother your lawyer or the courts about. Their resolution by lawyers would cost more than the damage done. “De minimis” is a Latin phrase the courts use to conceal their irritation at litigants who use the court’s time to solve the minor disputes of life.

Unless you are a deserving indigent, your lawyer isn’t interested in fighting for your principles at his expense. Intimidating him into doing so, for example, by suggesting you’ll get another lawyer, is to implant your unreasonableness in his mind. Pressuring your lawyer to embarrass himself before the court won’t help and may dampen his enthusiasm when, in fact, you need an enthusiastic champion for a really serious dispute.

A "QUICK LOOK" IS AS DANGEROUS AS OTHER QUICK ENCOUNTERS

A half-involved lawyer is like a half-pregnant woman - that is, non-existent. Once your lawyer has been engaged, he has undertaken a duty to you involving his full professional responsibility. If you ask him to "just take a quick look," "don't spend much time," you are like the seductive lover who proposes "a little fun."

Your lawyer's occasional willingness to accommodate you and take the risk, similar to accepting an unreasonably short deadline, may provide you with a short-term gratification, but ultimately will lead to mistakes or misunderstanding.

He knows from experience that when problems later arise because he had inadequate time to work out the correct solution to your problem, you may well have forgotten (or pretend to have forgotten) that you asked only for "a quick look."

You should understand when you make such a request that he does not want to incur either your annoyance or a later malpractice action. Avoid such requests if at all possible and if that's not possible, acknowledge in writing that you gave him such instructions.

MAY I CUT IN?

PARTIES ARE FOR PARTYING

You may think that you can get a quick answer from your lawyer at a party and, better still, get it free of charge. You may succeed. But not only is such a question a rude intrusion on his free time, but it runs the same risk of most quick questions and answers: over-simplification. Moreover, you may be interrupted or, heaven forbid, you or he may have had slightly too much to drink, so that what is communicated is only a partial answer. Worse still, you may construe it as a complete answer.

Do your talking to your lawyer in a quiet setting, preferably in his office or, if necessary, in your home. The law is replete with conditions, qualifications, exceptions, nuances and reservations. You need to hear and understand all of those that are relevant as well as the main point if your communications are to be effective.

FALSE STARTS - FALSE SAVINGS

It's not uncommon for you to first decide that you don't need a lawyer, that you can handle it yourself. Examples are do-it-yourself Wills, avoiding probate with form trusts, etc. or, worse still, real estate transactions and initiation of enterprises.

When you finally realize that you need a lawyer you don't hand him a clean slate but, by then, one that is a garbled mess. Undoing the mess, trying to identify the errors and pitfalls will often be more costly than seeing a lawyer in the first place.

At the very least, ask your lawyer in advance what specific aspects you can handle yourself and then follow his advice.

DEADLINES! DEADLINES! DEADLINES!

The law itself is full of deadlines and the process of handling your matter creates more. Some are hard and fast and some are more flexible, but still important.

Statutes of Limitation are critical. Miss those and your claim is useless. These statutes prescribe different periods in which a suit must be brought for different types of claims and the rules of application can be very complicated.

When you have any reason to believe that you may have a claim worth pursuing, don't hesitate to call your lawyer. Delay not only risks loss of your claim but puts your lawyer under pressure to take action immediately which, upon later reflection, might better have been avoided.

Give your lawyer the cooperation he needs to meet deadlines imposed by the law, by a court, specified in an agreement or simply needed to resolve your problem in a timely fashion.

MAP
LWR

GIVE YOUR LAWYER THE FACTS

Practicing lawyers, unlike law professors, deal with facts, not abstractions and hypotheticals. The facts, including, for purposes of fully explaining them, your opinions, evaluations and warnings regarding the facts, constitute the story you will want him to study, develop and act upon.

To the extent you gather and coherently present the facts and relevant data, you save him time and, therefore, save yourself fees. If you are unwilling or unable to assist in gathering facts or don't do it completely and accurately, expect your lawyer to charge you for doing it himself.

Once a conference date is set and he has checked and found no conflicts of interest (see below), mail any materials to him for review prior to the meeting. It will save time.

MAP

ALL THE FACTS

Get your money's worth by letting him decide what is, and is not, important to you. Withholding facts because you believe they "have nothing to do with it" can have the same effect as omitting your parents' heart attacks when giving your medical history to your doctor.

Relevance of facts to legal issues was central to your lawyer's education and is a subject about which he never ceases to learn. Understanding relevance may be the single most important reason your lawyer can do for you what you can't do for yourself, and why he is worth the fees you pay.

Proof is what a jury or judge thinks the evidence means. Your lawyer knows more about juries and judges than you do.

DETOUR
BRIDGE UNDER REPAIR
FOLLOW DETOUR

BEFORE IT IS TOO LATE

Facts can be embarrassing, demeaning or incriminating, but your lawyer must know them from the outset, not later, not after the contract has been signed, the case tried, a position announced in a negotiation. They are worse than useless then, generating frustration over what might have been.

Ask your lawyer before you sign - or expect to pay for your mistakes. You've surely heard that advice before.

GIVE YOUR LAWYER TIME TO USE THE BRAIN YOU'RE PAYING FOR

Giving your lawyer a short deadline is like giving a tailor two days in which to make a suit. You may get the suit, but it won't fit and it won't last - especially if the tailor has four other such orders at the same time.

Lawyers' thought processes usually involve scanning many possibilities and contingencies, sorting out their relevance, evaluating the personalities involved, selecting the best course from among various options and research and drafting. These processes as to your matter are invariably interrupted by other clients who want to talk about their matters. Your matter requires reflection and musing, as well as fact gathering, if the result is to work and last.

Alert him in advance, if possible, give him thinking time, make yourself available, have your thoughts and materials ready, complete and organized. When you recognize that he needs thinking time, you'll find him ready to work overtime.

STALE ADVICE, LIKE STALE BREAD, IS FOR THE BIRDS

The converse of not giving your lawyer enough time is giving him too much, which can be equally costly to you. Once a project is started and fresh in mind, to let it go stale is to invite wasted time and duplication when it resumes.

This is frequently done with wills and trusts. Once one begins to think seriously about his own departure from this world, it's easy to let happier subjects intrude. But when you call your lawyer six months after he sent you drafts (and three days before your vacation begins) expect to pay for some refreshing time and possibly a hurry-up job.

If it's your lawyer and not you who is delaying, let him know of your dissatisfaction. He owes you a duty of regular communication. If he does not respond to your complaints, get another lawyer.

URGENT DOCUMENT
GONE FISHIN'
BACK NEXT MONTH
Joe Client

TO KEEP YOUR LAWYER NEAR, LEND AN EAR

Despite all the high tech gadgets, clear communication with your lawyer still requires four ears, yours and his. If you have asked him to move ahead as quickly as possible and then you make yourself unavailable to answer the inevitable questions, don't expect rapid progress.

Let your lawyer know up front where, when and how you will be available for telephone calls and meetings. Is it okay for him to call you at home at night? On the weekends? Have you left a number at which you can be reached when out of town? Does he have your fax, cell and E-mail numbers?

If he can't reach you when he has the time, or at critical points, the effect can be as bad as your not being able to reach him.

I KNOW YOU SENT ME
A COPY.
I'M SURE IT'S RIGHT HERE.

TWO FILES ARE BETTER THAN ONE

It will expedite communication if you keep in your home or office a readily accessible, orderly file on your case or other legal matter, including letters and documents received from your lawyer. He will have copies of what he has sent you, but there are often telephone conversations which are facilitated by your having your copies in front of you.

Asking your lawyer to send another copy of a mislaid document may seem like a small matter to you, but to him it's another interruption along with many others in his busy day which soak up his time.

Gobbledygook
JUDGE

GOBBLEDYGOOK CAN BE GOLDEN

Everyone makes jokes about legal gobbledygook - except lawyers and judges. What seems to you to be legal gobbledygook is often a word or phrase that is time-honored by years of judicial interpretation. Lawyers know how a judge will treat a word or phrase because the law relies heavily on precedent; the interpretation given in the past will control in the future. Legal documents and arrangements serve you well when they express your interests so clearly, in the language of the law as well as in plain English, that no litigation ever becomes necessary, and if it does occur your version of the language's meaning prevails.

When your lawyer drafts a contract, corporate articles, will, trust, deed, lease, bond indenture, virtually any legal document, he is predicting how his language will be treated in court if it ever gets there. In that sense all legal advice is prognostication.

Predicting what the law will be and how it will be applied by a particular court years hence is difficult at best. Your patience with your lawyer's use of gobbledygook can save you future trouble and expense.

DID HE SAY I WAS SUPPOSED TO PULL SOMETHING?

DON'T "UNDERSTAND" IF YOU DON'T UNDERSTAND

Silence, nodding your head, asking no questions, deferring to a companion, makes your lawyer assume that you understand and acquiesce. Don't blame him later if he acts on that assumption. Far better to swallow your pride and risk embarrassment. Tell him that you don't get it, ask questions, disagree if necessary.

Confusion and disagreement expressed after the fact just creates more problems for your lawyer, sometimes irremediable. You are paying him to make difficult subjects absolutely clear to you. Don't mislead him into thinking that he has done his job when he hasn't.

RING
FAX

HIGH-TECH MEANS HIGH TENSION

Faster action started with the fax machine, if not the telephone, and now it's a curse as well as a blessing.

If you insist on fax, e-mail or computer communications with your lawyer, realize that you're often shortening his thinking time e.g., his need to mull over the provisions of a draft document he has just sent you. Lawyers are frequently asked, for example, promptly to send a draft document to a client for review. If sent by mail, the lawyer knows that he will have a few days (and nights) to check new case decisions or to mull over the terms and think of needed additions or subtractions which can be made before it is signed.

Where thinking time is crucial, insistence on using electronic exchanges (keeping in mind that you're not the only client doing it) can shrink thinking time drastically, resulting in risky documents being prematurely signed.

Confine such communication to situations where it is truly helpful and convenient and won't run the risk of eliminating essential thinking time.

CONTRACT
WE'LL WORK IT OUT LATER

DIFFERENCES DEFERRED ARE DICEY

When you are trying to work out an agreement, the temptation is to avoid discussing knotty details likely to cause disagreement. You assume that you can work those out later. But your lawyer knows that such details often cause serious friction and can lead to lawsuits.

Generally it is far better to work out potential problems with an adversary when both parties are in a friendly frame of mind and want to get the agreement signed, rather than count on being able to resolve them later. Let your lawyer be your guide. He will be able to advise you on the consequences of your delay, of not being able to resolve the issue later. He'll help you decide whether that eventuality is worth the risk of not resolving it up front.

GREASE

THE SQUEAKING CLIENT GETS GREASED, AT THE LEAST

If your lawyer isn't busy, begin to wonder if you have chosen the right lawyer. But remember that the practice of law is very demanding of him personally – it is a "hands-on" profession and many aspects of it often do not lend themselves to delegation to subordinates.

Nevertheless, once he agrees to do your work, you are entitled to have it done promptly and efficiently. Discuss in advance how much time he anticipates it will take to conclude the various stages of your work. Call him periodically to check on progress. That makes you a squeaking wheel and usually will result in action.

If unreasonable delays occur, ask him for an explanation and a time schedule you can count on. If delays continue without satisfactory explanation, tell him that you are going elsewhere.

"LET ME TELL YOU WHAT I TOLD MY LAWYER."

DON'T BLOW THE PRIVILEGE

By statute, you have the "privilege" of communicating with your lawyer in absolute secrecy, i.e., neither you nor he can be required to testify or otherwise reveal what you have expressed to your lawyer in confidence. Only you can waive that privilege. In other words the privilege is yours, not your lawyer's. But the privilege can be inadvertently waived by your discussing the same subject with persons other than your lawyer. You may thus blow the privilege without intending to do and make your statements vulnerable to disclosure in a deposition or trial.

To avoid a potential disaster, don't discuss the confidential aspects of your legal problem with anyone, or in the presence of anyone, other than your lawyer.

It may be that statements made in confidence to your lawyer are not important to your case and may be discussed with others without undue risk. But don't decide that on your own. Let your lawyer decide if the privilege is important in your particular situation.

Not so Good
News

SHOOTING THE MESSENGER PROVIDES ONLY TEMPORARY SATISFACTION

When your lawyer happens to be the messenger who brings you bad news, it does not mean that:

1. He's glad about it; or
2. He likes your adversary; or
3. He thinks it's fatal to your case; or
4. He thinks your version is wrong.

It's essential to consider the bad with the good in any legal problem. It's part of your lawyer's job to weigh them both. Intimidating your lawyer because he tells you things you don't want to hear only tends to chill a source of information you need.

Others with whom you consult often don't have all the facts or don't fully understand the law. Your lawyer usually is the only source of a fully informed, balanced opinion that you have. You need to discuss the bitter and the sweet with him in a calm, rational manner.

WHINER
HYPOCRITE
CHISELER
COWARD

TAKE ADVANTAGE OF HIS EXPERIENCE; HE SEES ALL KINDS

Unless his practice has been very narrowly specialized, your lawyer will be able to help you understand and deal with a variety of human types and qualities, each of which requires a slightly different approach, e.g., chiselers, cowards, heros, risk takers, piousness, frauds, sophisticates, boldness, timidity, stoicism, whiners, misers, philanthropists, gratitude, cheats, graciousness, naivete, cynics, trustworthiness, skeptics, optimists, pessimists, generosity, stinginess, sanctimoniousness, fools, idealists, realists, hypocrites, pragmatists.

Discuss the personalities of your adversaries with him. Don't be surprised if he is cynical. He seldom, if ever, will have encountered an altruist. The Mother Theresas of this world don't need lawyers. But, if he does encounter an altruist, your lawyer will usually recognize such an exception.

A TIME TO SHOUT; A TIME TO SEDUCE

Negotiation, like many interactions in life, often involves acting, whether you like it or not. Your lawyer knows how and when to control anger and how and when to use it; he knows that, like any tool, anger loses its edge from overuse.

Acting as if he is a tough, mean S.O.B. doesn't mean that he is, or that his fellow lawyers think he is. Conversely, cool, calm, objective analysis doesn't mean that he can't be an S.O.B. when you need an S.O.B. on your side.

Discussing negotiating tactics in advance will enable both of you to carry them out effectively.

UH-OH
I THINK I'LL HELP OUT!

DON'T CUT OFF THE LIMB YOU'RE BOTH SITTING ON

Unless advised otherwise, when you and your lawyer are meeting with your adversary, let your lawyer do the talking. If his maneuvering confuses or frustrates you, give him a chance to explain, in private, what he is trying to accomplish.

Overriding him in the presence of your adversary may make you feel in charge, but it often is done at the expense of destroying your lawyer's careful strategy that you may not fully comprehend.

Needless to say you should not communicate with your adversary except with your lawyer's express permission.

If your differences with your lawyer are real and unresolvable, tell him so in private and get another lawyer.

TWO MASTERS - TOO RISKY

You are entitled to your lawyer's loyalty. But conflicts, or potential conflicts, of interest occur. For example, you ask your lawyer to represent you in a claim against a debtor who has more debts than assets and it turns out that another claimant is represented by another lawyer in your lawyer's firm. That usually means his firm should not represent either you or the other claimant, sometimes leaving you high and dry when you need him the most. In some situations these can be finessed by written consents from all interested parties, but sometimes they cannot.

Rebuking your lawyer won't help. The rules of professional responsibility prohibit him from proceeding with such a conflict of interest.

To avoid delays, advise your lawyer on your first call of any actual or potential adverse parties of which you are aware. He'll quickly check with his firm as to possible conflicts.

COMMISSION
ON
GRIEVANCES
AND
DISCIPLINE

YOUR LAWYER MUST FACE GOD AND THE COMMISSION ON GRIEVANCES AND DISCIPLINE

You're entitled to your lawyer's loyalty - not his soul. Pressuring your lawyer to find a way to justify the stretching of the law is like asking your doctor to falsify your stress test. While he is not your moral advisor, the law and morals, at least sometimes, coincide and he is your predictor of legal consequences.

Once you corrupt his own conscience, his predictions become less reliable. His own meal ticket, i.e., his license to practice law, is at stake. He who enters into a conspiracy climbs into bed with a potential enemy, and the lawyer knows it. He also is acutely aware of the value of a good reputation - yours as well as his own.

This does not mean that taking an aggressive position with respect to an unclear law is never justified. It often is. But it should be done openly and with full disclosure of the relevant facts.

THE COURTHOUSE STEPS ARE THERE TO KEEP YOU OUT OF THE COURTHOUSE

The vast majority of legal disputes (say, 95%) are settled short of actual trial, most often by lawyers. Contrary to myth and all the jokes, most lawyers resort to courtroom trials only as the last, and highly undesirable, resort. That does not mean that lawsuits should seldom be filed. Post-filing, pre-trial discovery such as depositions are often the only means of revealing the truth.

The psychological pressure of an imminent trial date works wonders on the willingness of clients and lawyers alike to get realistic about resolving their differences before a judge or jury does it for them. That's why the courthouse steps are there.

In evaluating your settlement options, remember to consider these truisms.

ARBITRATOR

LITIGATION IS NOT THE ONLY WAY

A law suit, i.e., litigation, is not the only way to resolve a dispute. In fact, it is often a slow, expensive, frustrating, stressful way to do it. The judicial system has long recognized those simple facts and encourages use of various alternatives:

1. Arbitration - a method of "trial" with far simpler rules than litigation, conducted by an impartial Arbitrator, whose decision is binding on the parties, with no right of appeal to the courts.

2. Mediation - conducted by an independent Mediator who helps the parties reach a settlement. It is a non-binding process until an agreement is made.

3. Collaborative Law - a negotiation whereby the parties and their respective lawyers have agreed that if a party withdraws before resolution and decides on litigation, the lawyers will withdraw and not represent anyone in the litigation, i.e. that new counsel will be retained.

Your lawyer can advise as to which of these alternatives best suits your situation and he can help you through the process.

LAWYER #2

BETTER TO HURT YOUR LAWYER'S FEELINGS THAN YOUR CASE

Don't hesitate to tell your lawyer what you don't like about his performance, but do it constructively. Properly done, it will help clear the air and give him a better idea as to how to serve you. No one knows better than he does that he owes you a fiduciary duty to serve your interests to the best of his ability. Moreover, he knows that the lawyer-client relationship is intensely personal and that differences with his clients, whether of personality or of methods, must be resolved.

Effective representation can only be achieved in an atmosphere of respect and trust. If that is lacking, the solution may be to use another lawyer in the same firm or to terminate the relationship entirely. When the latter becomes necessary, don't just disappear. Tell him candidly why you are leaving. He wants to know how and why he's failed.

If your dissatisfaction relates to fees, ask to see his time records and review your file with you. If you still don't understand, or seriously object to his fees, and discussion doesn't resolve your differences, seek mediation or arbitration or, as a last resort, litigation.

Whatever the issue, he should help in expediting your transfer to new counsel and in delivering your file information. That process will be facilitated by your handling the transfer in as courteous a manner as is possible.

IT WON'T HURT TO BE NICE TO YOUR LAWYER

Don't be surprised if you discover that your lawyer will respond to respect and consideration just as any normal human being does.

Treat your lawyer as a full-time member of a learned profession, duty bound to serve your best interests, and he'll respond as a full time member of a learned profession duty bound to serve your best interests.

He is trying to work effectively while making the most of his time. If he knows that you are trying to help him to do just that (for example, by paying heed to the other advice in this book) he will try even harder to make sure you remain a happy client.

APPENDIX

Canons of Professional Responsibility

The conduct of lawyers is governed by each state in which they are licensed, generally by rules promulgated by the highest court of that state. In Ohio, for example, the Supreme Court of Ohio has issued the CODE OF PROFESSIONAL RESPONSIBILITY which includes nine Canons. The Canons are statements of general concepts. In addition, there are elaborate Ethical Considerations, which are aspirational and state objectives toward which every lawyer should strive, and mandatory Disciplinary Rules with respect to each Canon. The Code is reviewed and revised periodically, often in light of changes proposed in the Model Rules of Professional Responsibility published by the American Bar Association.

The Ohio Code is enforced by the Ohio Board of Commissioners on Grievances and Discipline. Copies of the entire Code may be obtained from the Ohio State Bar Association 1700 Lakeshore Drive P.O. Box 16562 Columbus, Ohio 43216-6562.

The Ohio Canons, for example, are as follows:

CANON 1. A lawyer should assist in maintaining the integrity and competence of the legal profession.

CANON 2. A lawyer should assist the legal profession in fulfilling its duty to make legal counsel available.

CANON 3. A lawyer should assist in preventing the unauthorized practice of law.

CANON 4. A lawyer should preserve the confidences and secrets of a client.

CANON 5. A lawyer should exercise independent professional judgment on behalf of a client.

CANON 6. A lawyer should represent a client competently.

CANON 7. A lawyer should represent a client zealously within the bounds of the law.

CANON 8. A lawyer should assist in improving the legal system.

CANON 9. A lawyer should avoid even the appearance of professional impropriety.

CAVEAT EMPTOR[2]

This booklet is not intended as legal advice. It is only an aid to you in securing effective legal assistance and in minimizing your cost of legal services. Some lawyers are more responsive and attentive than others; in some cases nothing you can do seems to help, but most lawyers work hard to give you the results you want.   These suggestions will help with most lawyers.

[2] "Let the buyer beware" - an old doctrine, somewhat dated, but still useful, especially when you're buying.

THANKS

For their friendly suggestions, constructive criticism and welcome comments, I gratefully thank friends and colleagues, many of whom are lawyers, who have generously given their time to help with this booklet. They especially include Marjorie Fox, Drew Gores, Mary Gough, Michael Hirschfeld, Joseph Jaap, Robert Kriedler, Richard LaJeunesse, Norman Levy, Robert Marriott, Joan Mayer, William Parker, Terry Patterson, Bruce Petrie Jr., Janice Pogue and Marnie Streit. Needless to say, any mistakes are my own.

Bruce I. Petrie

Bruce I. Petrie is a member and former President of The Cincinnati Bar Association, a member of the American and Ohio State Bar Associations, recipient of the Ohio Bar Medal, the Distinguished Alumnus Award of the University of Cincinnati College of Law and other professional honors.

Donald R. Heyl is a professional graphic designer, freelance cartoonist and the Design Director of The National Underwriter Company of Erlanger, Kentucky.

NOTES

ORDER FORM

FAX ORDERS: 513-321-1601
TELEPHONE: 513-321-2771

POSTAL ORDERS: SAPIOZOIC PRESS, 2787 WALSH ROAD, CINCINNATI, OHIO 45208

PLEASE SEND _______ COPIES OF

How To Get The Most Out Of Your Lawyer

PLEASE PRINT:

NAME ____

ADDRESS ____

CITY ____________________ STATE ____________ ZIP ________

TELEPHONE ____

PLEASE ADD 6% SALES TAX FOR BOOKS SHIPPED TO OHIO ADDRESS
SHIPPING AND HANDLING: PLEASE ADD $1.75 per book.
For larger orders please call.
PAYMENT: BY CHECK OR U.S. CURRENCY

QUANTITY DISCOUNTS AVAILABLE